TA |||||||||||||||||||||||||||||
D0596632

Introduction

Are you stuck in a job that you can't stand? Sick of your boss making far more money than you for doing far less work? Tired of making sacrifices because you never have any extra money at the end of the month?

If you can relate to any of these feelings, I want you to know that there is a better way to work. There is a way to work the hours you want, with whomever you want, and earn as much income as you want. It takes very little money to get started, and there is no formal experience required.

How is this possible?

Believe it or not, network marketing is the vehicle that can make all of this possible if you apply the principles outlined in the following chapters. But before you put this book down because of a bad experience you or a friend had in this industry, do me a favor and forget everything you've ever heard or thought about MLMs up until now and hear me out— network marketing is not the business it once was.

Once upon a time this was an industry where cold calling and soliciting strangers were the primary forms of finding prospects and it was nearly impossible to succeed. You were forced to harass family and friends in a desperate attempt to push your products, and most people quit before they even made a single paycheck. It was a time when connecting with people outside your local area was difficult, and many people suffered from their inability to connect.

Don't get me wrong, there are still people who operate their business in the ways I just described, but that's because they don't know any better. Our systems still encourage you to share your products with people you know, but your business will not rely on those people alone because today's era of technology opens up the playing field to a whole new level. This book is going to show you how to work smarter than all of your competitors and build a business that thrives while you're relaxing by the beach with the people you love.

With no prior experience in sales and very little knowledge of the industry, my business partner, Denise, and I both managed to create a 7-figure annual income in just a few short years using the tools, exercises and resources laid out for you in this book. We are the top two money earners in our company because we created a system for success that anyone can learn and duplicate for their own direct sales business.

Wouldn't it be great if you could "fire" your boss so you could start earning the kind of money you deserve for the hard work you're already doing? So you could spend less time "crunching numbers" and more time making memories with your family?

If you can commit a couple hours of your time to reading this book and completing the exercises within it, I know you can retire your husband (and/or yourself) in 2 years or less. Sure, you can wait to read this book when you "feel like it," but the longer you wait, the more likely it is that your dreams will stay just that—dreams.

If you're sick of wishing for a better life and hoping your luck will turn around, turn the page to find out how you can make your wildest dreams a reality with our unique systems for success. I know you won't regret it.

one.

WHAT DOES RETIRING YOUR HUSBAND REALLY MEAN?

"The best way to predict the future is to create it."
—Peter Drucker

written by ***DENISE WALSH***

Congratulations!

You've just taken the first step toward building (or re-building) your business, which means you're already closer to creating the future you've always wanted for you and your family. This chapter will tell you exactly what it really means to retire your husband and how you can use your business to create a legacy of wealth and freedom for years to come. If you want to know how I went from making 5 figures a year and hating my job to making 6 figures a month and loving every day, keep reading and you'll find out very soon...

Ever since I was a little girl, my passion has been helping people. I know that's a cliché thing to say, but my past is proof of this passion. From church groups to summer camps to social work, I thought I had everything figured out by the time I graduated college. What you'll soon learn, however, is that I found my dream life in a business I never expected to be in.

If you picked up this book, you (or your partner) are probably wondering what it means to "retire your husband." And, in a nutshell, it means freedom. Freedom for you, your husband, and your family. It means choices before sacrifices and it means more time for your kids and passions. It means getting paid whether you go to work or not. Really, retiring your husband is exactly what you want it to mean, because it's all about designing your dream life and putting it into motion.

Designing Your Dream Life

How do you make your so-called dream life a reality? Two words: residual income. Residual income is money that you earn over and over and over again—and the best part is... it all comes from a single investment. This kind of income is more difficult to create initially, but it is, without a doubt, the key to freedom with your family, finances, and time.

If you aren't familiar with the concept of residual income, think about it like this—when J.K. Rowling wrote the infamous Harry Potter series, she wasn't paid a lump some at the end of every book she finished and sent home afterward. Instead, she made an investment in herself and her work and got paid for it gradually over time.

Even though it has been more than a decade since the first Harry Potter book was released, Rowling is still getting paid for it. She's also getting paid for the six books after that. And the seven movies after that. And the countless masses of memorabilia and merchandise after that. In short, her work is done, but her paychecks are not.

What If I'm Not J.K. Rowling?

Unlike J.K. Rowling, you expect to be paid each week upon working a set number of hours. This also means you're trading your time for money. Now, don't get me wrong, this kind of exchange is essential for our economy and perfectly fine for part-time work and people who truly love their careers. For some of us, however, our jobs are just that—a job, something you do in order to keep food on the table. These everyday, unfulfilling "jobs" are what I'm arguing against. There is a better way to work.

Realistically, I know we're not all famous authors, movie-makers and musicians who can just crank out creative masterpieces and get paid on them for the rest of our lives. What I do know, though, is that there are other ways to create residual income—ways that are accessible and affordable to the general public.

For me, the solution was in direct sales. Earlier I said I found my dream life in a business I never expected to be in, but I can honestly say that I have made a greater difference in people's lives in the last six years of building my own business than I did in all my years as a therapist.

When I was in college studying to become a therapist, I was excited to learn more about psychology and how I could eventually make a positive impact on the people around me. This desire led me to graduate school, where I was excited to master my skills and soon put them into action. When I finally graduated college and got my first real job at a local mental health agency, I was beyond excited to see how all of my hard work would pay off in an environment where I could exercise all the skills I spent so much time practicing.

But, as you might expect, it wasn't long before I grew tired of the paperwork and politics of the corporate world. Things were fine at first; I felt like I was doing the job that was expected of me, I was getting paid, and my bosses didn't scowl at me too much. I was content for a while, but I knew I wasn't helping people the way I imagined I could. Many individuals were sent to me by court orders, and therefore were people who didn't really want my help.

Not only that, but as time went on, my caseload increased while budgetary cuts slashed my hours simultaneously. With only a few years in the field, I felt stuck. I did my best to stay optimistic and tell myself I was making a difference, but my husband soon chimed in with the frustrations of his own cubicle life. We were both dumbfounded—how did our so-called dream jobs turn out to be such nightmares? Though we were only in our mid-20s at the time, we knew we were ready to get out of the corporate world. We were lucky to realize this as early as we did because there are so many people out there who keep jobs they hate solely because they don't know what else they'd do.

Do your bosses appreciate you? Are you fulfilled by your job? I think these are questions worth asking yourself—if you're not happy with where you're at, there are other options.

My husband, Brandon, always dreamt of being an entrepreneur, but the security of a salary as a systems engineer seemed too good to pass up when he had thousands in student loans to pay off. We stayed complacent in our post-college careers for a few years because we were doing pretty well when a lot of other families we knew were not. So, in an effort to feel safe in an unstable economy, we sacrificed true satisfaction in our work.

Needless to say, when a friend in our church group approached us about a new business she was building, we were both eager to hear more.

Kami, my mentor and the co-author of this book, introduced us to the company she was getting involved in and what it was all about. By the time she finished giving us the "spiel," my husband and I were reeling for more. We knew we could trust Kami and her husband Nathan to be honest about the opportunity and we loved the unique products and unrestricted schedule it offered. We were hoping to have a child soon and couldn't help imagining how wonderful life would be if both of us could work from home.

I know some people are immediately skeptical when they hear about others being successful in direct sales or network marketing because of its stigmas as a pyramid scheme or get rich quick scam, but the fact of the matter is, people are successful in this industry all the time. Success comes to the people who never forget why they started and the people who stick it out through the difficult times— the nos, the negativity, the hang ups, and everything else that makes the others quit. These people never give up because they know that ultimately, if you do it right and work your tail off, a career in direct sales leads to a future of complete freedom.

In fact, it was just this past January that I was in Florida with my husband for our company's annual conference and we were brought on stage for being one of two couples to make a million dollars in commissions in the last year. The other couple was Kami and Nathan Dempsey, who were also completely new to all of this. I don't tell you this to brag about our accomplishments, but to show you that it can be done. Not only that, but anyone can do it. Our hope is that by sharing our story—the ups, the downs and everything in between, you'll get all the information and advice you need to be successful in your own network marketing business.

So if you're as intrigued and excited by this concept of residual income as I was six years ago, I believe we can give you the tools you need to retire your husband and begin living the life of your dreams. It wasn't so long ago that I was stuck in a cubicle working a job I thought I would love. But when an opportunity came knocking at my less-than-content door, you better believe I was ready to answer.

When you're ready to take on this opportunity to build your own business and design your dream life, I know Kami and I can show you the steps to success. It's not going to be easy work, and there are definitely times that you'll be so frustrated that you'll want to quit. But some of you will stick with it and succeed because you'll come to understand that the life ahead of you is worth all the hard work in the world.

Now that you understand just how powerful residual income can be and how you can achieve it in this industry, we're going to dive into the next chapter where Kami will explain why the stereotypes of network marketing are just plain wrong. She'll also give you some insider info on how to choose the perfect company and how to get past some of the most common obstacles that stop people from succeeding in this business before they even start.

Shall we dig in?

two.

IS NETWORK MARKETING THE ANSWER TO MY PROBLEMS?

"Choose a job you live, and you will never work a day in your life."
—*Confucius*

written by **KAMI DEMPSEY**

In the introduction of this book, Denise pointed out the sometimes controversial nature of the words, "networking marketing," "direct sales" and/or "multi-level marketing." Because most of us have been introduced to one of these companies or its products through a relative, friend, or co-worker, it's easy to dismiss this business model as a scam if that person didn't succeed with the business— after all, most people fail to make any real money in network marketing anyway, right? Right. This chapter is going to explain why most people fail to build a successful and long-lasting direct sales business, and what you can do to avoid these often-overlooked pitfalls right off the bat.

The Problem With MLM

The underlying problem with direct sales is not direct sales. The stigmas of this industry stem from the people who act on an impulse and sign up to become a representative without thinking about the long-term commitment of building (and maintaining) your own business. Instead of doing their homework and coming up with a game plan for launching their new business, these impulse-entrepreneurs see an opportunity to "get rich quick" and their eyes suddenly glaze over with dollar signs and dreams of life by the beach. Then, when they're 6 months into the business and haven't seen a paycheck they're happy with, they deem the whole thing a scam and quit.

Even if you've never tried your hand at networking marketing, we're all guilty of failing at something we were once excited about accomplishing. I'm sure all of us can relate to this when we think back to some of those not-so-successful New Year's Resolutions we've made throughout our lives. Regardless of your resolution's nature (eat better, quit smoking, exercise more, etc.), it's always easier to get excited than it is to stay excited.

Just as the majority of people give up on their resolutions within the first month of making them, most people quit network marketing within the first three months of signing up. The reason most people give up their New Year's Resolutions so quickly is because they weren't really passionate about their goals in the first place. If you truly desired to eat better this year and wanted to accomplish that more than anything else, you wouldn't have given in at the first sign of free donuts. It's really the same concept with network marketing—if you just "want to earn a residual income," like you "want to eat better," it's probably not going to happen. But, if you truly want to succeed in direct sales and live a life of fun and freedom, so much so that it plagues your every thought and you won't stop until you get there— you're in the right place!

How to Succeed in Direct Sales

When my husband, Nathan, and I first got involved with direct sales, we were in the middle of a very difficult time financially. Both of us were teachers/coaches in our local public school system and we were having a hard time making ends meet at the end of each month. We made it work for a while because we loved what we were doing, but once I got pregnant with my first son and I was on sabbatical with no paycheck, we knew something had to change.

Needing another way to supplement our fixed, single income with little free time to spare and even less money to invest, there wasn't exactly a long list of options available to us. Real estate? Too expensive. Stocks? Too risky. Another job? Too inflexible. After a lot of consideration, we decided to give networking marketing a shot. Because my dad had been successful in the industry, we didn't need any convincing that network marketing was a legitimate way to make money—we just needed to find the right "vehicle" for us. We did research on a number of businesses, but there was one company that really stood out to us. We saw the amazing potential, scrounged up the initial investment required for the business kit, and started strategizing.

Because my father always had a "How to Succeed in Business" book on his desk and a dream to make it big with network marketing, his advice on choosing the perfect company really impacted our journey to success. Aside from doing some basic research on the company in question, one important thing I learned from my dad was the formula to choosing that perfect "vehicle." When you're researching businesses for yourself, keep these key questions at the forefront of your mind—

> *Do they have a standalone product or service that is unique aand competitively priced?—Are their products or services in demand by a large number of people? Is it a consumable product—one that they will use over and over again?*

> *What is the potential of their compensation plan?—Is there a cap to how much I can earn? What bonuses do they offer? How does this plan compare to others in the industry? How much are the top leaders in this company earning?*

> *How does this company measure success?—Do they value team success or is it all about the individual?*

> *How is the timing of this company compared with current trends?—Are they offering a luxury product in a time of economic hardship? Will this product or service maintain its "wow" factor over time?*

Once we had been working our business for about six months, we started to see some real "fruits" from our labor as we signed up new teammates and were slowly gaining momentum. Our checks weren't much in that first year of getting started, but they definitely made a positive impact on our paycheck-to-paycheck lifestyles. Before we had any of this extra money coming in, our fixed salaries as teachers forced us to spend a lot of time budgeting and making compromises on our expenses to make sure we had enough for our mortgage. If we spent $45 on a hair clipping set, we knew we could save about $15 every month on haircuts. We didn't exactly know how to cut hair, but we had to cut corners (or in this case, hairs) somehow. So, even though those checks from our new business were small to start, we were seeing more choices and making fewer sacrifices in our every day lives. The seed of residual income had been planted in our bellies and we were hungry for more.

Really, we never stopped being hungry—we kept talking to new people, organizing new events, sharing our story and growing our business. And, within a few short years, our lives had completely changed—we had two more beautiful children and we were no longer struggling to pay our mortgage. We finally had money in our savings, we were designing our dream home, and we were both working from home.

Once we got in a position to help people who were stuck like us, it became our mission. Because Nathan and I were in a pretty rough place in our lives not so many years ago, we know how it feels to want something different for yourself, your family, and your future. We wanted to leave a legacy of freedom for our family and we knew we couldn't do that if we didn't take action to change something. So, even though I had no formal experience selling anything except for Girl Scout Cookies and lemonade, I did it anyway! We didn't question or doubt ourselves despite our lack of experience—in our minds, it wasn't a question of "if" we make this work, it was "when." Nathan and I have only been involved with one network marketing company, but we are proud to say that we are currently the number one money earners in that company, earning six figures and up every month.

We initially got involved in this business because we needed the extra income, but the more we learned, the more we grew, and the more we loved. When I look back on where we were five years ago and where we are today, I know we were in the right place at the right time—and we acted on it, even though there were plenty of reasons we could have failed.

I didn't know how I was going to sell these products to a bunch of people I didn't know, but I knew it had to be done. That frame of my mind really reinforces the point that Denise made earlier: Anyone can be successful in this business if they want it badly enough. I was a teacher with no experience in sales or marketing and I had no idea who to bring this new business to, but I started talking to strangers anyway. I started building relationships. I started listening to people—truly listening to people and seeing what their needs were. Sometimes my product helped them, sometimes it didn't—but I was always building new relationships with people.

Today I feel like this job is truly a part of God's purpose for me— as a former athlete and former teacher/coach, this role of leadership was a natural fit once I realized how I could apply it to my new business. I spent many years developing those skills through various jobs and hobbies, and now I put them to work every day as I help inspire people around the world who want to change their futures. I am very humbled and blessed to be able to share my story and teach others how to do what we have done. There's nothing different about Nathan and I or Denise and Brandon that have made us successful in this business except that we took action at the right time and put our unique skill sets to work. We made an investment in ourselves and now we are looking to help others who want to do the same thing. One of the aspects I love most about this industry is the opportunity to build meaningful relationship with others, regardless of what you can get from them in return. But the truth is (and Zig Ziglar said it best)—*"You can have everything in life you want, if you will just help other people get what they want."*

I know Denise and I would be honored to help you along in your journey to live your best life, but before we can truly dive into the specifics of our strategy, it's really important that you know why you want to do this. To succeed as an entrepreneur, you have to be extremely proactive and know that your every day efforts in building this business are what's going to make you or break you. There won't be a certain time you need to wake up in the morning or anyone hovering over you to make sure you're working, so you need to be self-motivated and willing to step out of your comfort zone often. You will do things you've never done, talk to people you never thought you would, and achieve things you never thought possible. *It will be very difficult AND very rewarding,* but you will succeed if you keep the right mindset in place.

Hopefully you now know why so many people fail in this industry right away, how you can avoid those mistakes, and what you should look for when it's time for you to choose a company of your own. I know this is a lot of information at once, but I want to prepare you with all the information and tools you need to get started right away!

The next chapter is going to help you form the mindset you *need to succeed* in this business. It might seem insignificant now, but countless people quit this industry solely because they weren't mentally prepared for the journey ahead. This industry will require you to work hard, but it will also allow you to have more fun than you ever imagined. If you follow along with the next chapter, we're going to show you some great exercises you can do today to get your head in the right place for massive success in your future.

three.

HOW DO I FIND MY PASSION?

"The most powerful weapon on earth is the human soul on fire."
—Ferdinand Foch

written by **DENISE WALSH**

Have you ever wanted something so badly that it hurt? ...So much that it drowned out all of your other thoughts and kept you awake at night? ...So much that you would do anything in your power to make it happen?

If you answered yes, you already know what it means to have a fire in your belly. But even if you know what it means to have one, you probably don't know just how important that passion is to this business. This chapter is extremely important to anyone who is seriously considering starting a new MLM business or someone who is looking to get back into the industry after a bad experience in the past because it will help you outline exactly what you want out of this business, and how you can use those desires to fuel your every day efforts. If you don't take the time to identify your "why" now, you may never do it—and that's almost a certain recipe for failure. Keep reading and keep following along with the exercises, and you will be in a great position to launch your business within the next few days.

What is the Fire?

The fire in your belly is a humanly force that cannot be reckoned with—it's a deep-rooted desire for change, and it doesn't come from the weak-willed. It comes from strong beliefs, amazing causes, and paralyzing passions.

This fire is fueled by big dreams and it's always hungry for more. Most fires can be put out with water or strong winds—this fire cannot. This flame cannot die because it's not driven by fleeting results like money or fame. It burns day in and day out because it's driven by passion and purpose. This fire may evolve over time—it may burn brighter and hotter as the belief grows stronger, but it never dies.

Why Do I Need A Fire In My Belly?

When Kami first introduced me to this business, I knew exactly why I was doing it—I no longer wanted to be tied down to a 9-5 job, regardless of my salary, because I didn't want to trade my time for money anymore. I wanted the freedom to make choices and plans as I saw fit, the freedom to work when and where I wanted, and the freedom to spend more time at home with my family. I didn't know I'd want these things in college, but after a few years of working in the "real world," I realized how challenging the traditional workplace could be— the early mornings, late nights, mountains of paperwork, looming budgetary cuts, office politics, and case after case of clients who "needed" my help but didn't want it made it difficult to find real satisfaction in my work.

My day-to-day life in the office was nothing like I pictured it would be. When I first met Kami and she presented me with this opportunity to get "out," I was incredibly eager to learn and get started. Even though I had never thought of network marketing as a viable career path for myself, I knew it was worth a shot if it meant I could ultimately leave my full-time job forever. I doubted myself a lot in those first few months, wondering what I was thinking getting into a business that I had no business being in (or so I thought). There were so many times that I picked up my phone ready to call Kami and tell her I quit, but something stopped me every time. Something deep down inside of me told me to keep going— I had to make this business work if I wanted to escape my cubicle for good.

If you want to become an entrepreneur, you absolutely, without a doubt, NEED that feeling deep down inside of you telling you to keep going to be successful—it's the fuel that keeps you motivated to work when you want to give up most. Without it, there's very little chance you will succeed. I don't say this to discourage you, I say this because I've been in this business long enough to know how people work—and why they do or do not fail.

Generally speaking, humans operate their day-to-day activities for one of two reasons—

1 | Because they're obligated to do so, or—

2 | Because they want to.

Think about it this way—if you're someone with a job in the traditional workplace (work 35-40 hours a week and receive a fixed income in return), you get out of bed every morning because you're obligated to get to work at a certain time. Once you get to work, you're obligated to complete any number of tasks assigned to you. If you fulfill all of your obligations in a given week, your boss is then obligated to pay you. If you don't fulfill all of your obligations, however, your boss does not have to pay you. In fact, he/she may even fire you. In the end, this feeling of obligation andfear of unwanted consequences is what keeps us waking up every morning and going to work.

But, if your boss was not obligated to pay you in any given week, regardless of whether you did your end of the work, would you still show up every morning? Probably not.

If you're someone who does not have a job in the traditional workplace, on the other hand, this routine plays out rather differently. Let's say you're an entrepreneur who has just joined a networking company because you heard from a friend that it's a great way to make some money. You get out of bed in the morning because you want to make money. You don't have a boss telling you how often you should work, so you work for a few hours... and that feels like enough, so you stop. A week of this passes, and you wonder how much income you've generated with your new business.

Monday morning rolls around yet again, so you get of bed because you still want to make money. You work for a few hours and hope that it's enough because you're already sick of working and you're wondering how all of this network marketing stuff really works. Another week passes, and still, no paycheck. This process continues for a couple more weeks, and then a month, and you still haven't made a single cent. So, what do you do? You quit. You quit because you no longer have any motivation to keep going. Your motivation to start was to make money, and because you worked for a month and made no money, your motivation ran out. It was a fling.

Now let's say that you are another entrepreneur, one who has just joined a network marketing company because you recently had your first child and couldn't bear to put them in daycare all week while you were working your 9-5 office job. Your fear of leaving your teary-eyed baby at daycare to be raised by someone else is a thought that would haunt you all day long—it's much stronger than a simple "it's nice to be working at home."

You get out of bed in the morning and want to get to work right away because your baby is still asleep. You work for as long as you can before your baby needs you, and continue working after they've gone to bed because you know your opportunities to work are limited. When you get out of bed the next morning and see your baby sleeping in the crib in their room, you are reminded of how lucky you are to have them at home with you and not someone else. A few weeks of this goes by, but you still have no paycheck to show for it. So, what do you do? You keep going. You keep going because money was not your motivation, your baby was. Your baby fueled the fire in your belly and that fire kept you working. That work will pay off monetarily too, but because your "why" was stronger than just money, you were willing to work through those first few weeks without a paycheck unlike the entrepreneur whose main motivation was making money.

The biggest difference among entrepreneurs is what drives them to want to work. What kind of entrepreneur are you? Are you motivated by a fling, like money? Or is it a fire, like family?

Only you can decide.

How Do You Discover Your Fire?

Everyone's fire burns for a different reason, but everyone can find what fuels them when they start with the same question: Why?

Why do you want to become an entrepreneur and build a successful direct sales business?

If your answer is as simple as "to make more money" or "to drive a sports car," you need to dig deeper. If you want to make more money so you can get out of debt and have enough money to buy healthy organic groceries or top-notch schooling for your children, that's a different story because it's not just about money—it's about providing for your children and wanting to give them the best of the best.

In order to find the fire that burns deep within, there are a few exercises I'd like you to complete before we move on. Whenever I sign up a new team member, I give them these exercises as "homework" to complete before we talk again. I assign this homework right away because it establishes a frame of mind that will stick with you throughout the inevitable roller coaster of emotions you'll experience during your journey. If you're serious about becoming an entrepreneur and building your own network marketing business, I can't stress how important it is that you actually sit down and take the time to complete both of these exercises before continuing onto the next chapters. Let's get started!

Exercise 1—Create Your Ideal Day

Grab a pencil and pad of paper and set aside 15 minutes for this exercise right now and begin writing about your perfect day as if it just happened. Be very specific and include all the little details you can think of.

What time did you wake up? Where did you wake up—what did your bedroom or house or hotel look like? Who were you with? What was their attitude? What was yours? What did you have for breakfast? What was the weather like? Who were you with? Did you go anywhere? What kinds of things did you do? What did you talk about? Keep in mind this day can include anything, anyone, anywhere. It doesn't have include your family if you don't want it to... this is YOUR ideal day.

Once you've finished writing, take a minute to stop and reflect on what you wrote. Share it with others. What's stopping you from making every day an ideal day? What needs to change to make your ideal day possible? Is network marketing the right vehicle to make this happen?

If you do believe that network marketing is the vehicle that can make your dreams a reality, save this piece of paper and keep it by your bedside. Every night before you go to bed, read that piece of paper again. Add to it, if you want. Then, when you wake up in the morning, read it then too. It will take no more than a couple minutes out of each day, but it will serve as a constant reminder of what you're working toward and why you're working toward it. If you're not making conscious steps toward this ideal lifestyle, you're moving away from it.

Exercise 2—Design Your Dream Board

This exercise will put images and actions to the words that you just wrote down for the ideal day exercise. You'll need a poster board, some old magazines, scissors, markers, and glue.* Once you have the materials on hand, you can start looking through the magazines to find pictures and words that represent your goals. If you have a spouse, partner or other family member who plays an important part of your dreams, include them in this exercise and ask for their opinions too! The family that dreams together, stays together.

Tip: You can also create your dream board on the computer via Oprah's website http://www.oprah.com/spirit/O-Dream-Board-Envision-Your-Best-Life™

These images and words will serve as a daily reminder of your "why" checklist. If you write something out, be sure to write it in the present tense like it's happening right now. "I'm backpacking across Europe" or "We love being stay-at-home parents." Writing your dreams as if you're already living them helps you believe that it can happen—if you don't believe you can do it, you can't expect anyone else to.

Once you've filled your board, you should begin taking action steps (no matter how small they may seem) to move closer to your goals. If one of your dreams is a top tier school for your kids... what will that cost? Per year? Per month? Per day? How many new representatives will you have to recruit to get there? If this top tier school costs 100k a year, that's $8,333.33 a month, which is about $278 a day. Now how many people would you need in your organization to make that much every day? It might seem impossible to you right now; this goal might feel too big or too far out of your reach, but that's only because you haven't broken it down into enough small steps. If the task seems too big, make a plan of small, achievable action steps that will slowly lead you to your ultimate goal.

You should really envision yourself living your dreams and even say them out loud. "I love being on vacation in _____ with my family" or "Being debt-free relieves me of so much stress every day!"

After it's finished, keep your dream board in a visible area that you can see every day. Take a few minutes to imagine yourself living that life every morning and every night. If you give yourself a real chance to dream again by completing these exercises and taking the time to think about them every day, I think you'll be surprised by how much you get in return—not only will you instill this kind of lifestyle in your own mind, but you will also instill these values onto your children, family, and friends who visit your home. Everyone wants to dream, but not everyone has the courage to put their dreams out in the open. But, believe me—when you show others that you believe in yourself and that you deserve your dreams, you will simultaneously inspire others to do the same.

Now that you're prepared to take on any challenge or adversity that could possibly be thrown your way, we're going to jump right into the launch. The next couple chapters are going to give you the blueprint you need to successfully launch (or re-launch) your business in just 90 days. We'll give you some great exercises that you can get started with as soon as you read them to get your business off on the right track from day 1... ready, set, go!

four.

HOW DO I GET MY BUSINESS STARTED?

"Entrepreneurs are responsible for their own destiny. If things don't work out for them they have no one to blame but the person in the mirror. To some people that is frightening, to others it is exhilarating."

—Jim Randel
Author of The Skinny On Direct Sales: Your First 100 Days

written by ***KAMI DEMPSEY***

By now you know the common pitfalls to avoid, the formula for choosing the perfect company, and the tools you need to train your brain for long-term success. The next step in the process is getting out there and officially launching your business. This chapter will zero in on your first 30 days of launching and all the tasks you should be focusing your energy on, while the next chapter will focus on the second and third month of your launch. The relationships you form, habits you make, and routines you get into throughout the first 90 days will be absolutely crucial to your long-term success, so pay close attention to the contents of these next few chapters.

You might be wondering why Denise and I have spent so much time talking about how to prepare yourself mentally for building your own business—it's because we believe that your mindset in this business can singlehandedly shape your success. If you have a fire in your belly to fuel you, believe you can succeed and surround yourself with people who believe in you, you will not fail.

Now that you have a vision for the big picture in place, we're going to dive into the next most important part of your journey: the first 90 days.

The first 90 days of building your business are especially crucial because it's generally how long it takes people to figure out whether or not they're going to really commit to "making it" with network marketing. Those who don't make it, coincidentally, are the people who were not mentally prepared for the challenge, the discipline, or the commitment that is necessary to build (and maintain) your own business.

One thing I think is really significant to stress before you start talking to strangers about your business or products is the link between relationship building and success in this industry. Everyone is a potential customer, but that doesn't mean that everyone wants your product. Listen before you sell, always be respectful, and don't be discouraged when someone says no. The better you treat people, the more successful you will be in this industry. My teammates see me as a "real friend" because I genuinely care about them and their well-being whenever I talk to them—if you treat people how you would like to be treated, you really can't go wrong. The Golden Rule will always be true!

Even if someone does say no (and trust me, they will), it's important that you maintain a relationship with that person. It may be a no right now, but it might be a yes in a few months or a yes for someone else they know and want to refer to you. You never know when someone will surprise you when their circumstances change and they remember the relationship you've formed. I know Denise approached her cousin, Nikki, about the business not too long after launching and Nikki said that she was interested in the concept of the industry, but she wasn't in the best position to get involved right away. Two years later, Nikki was the one to approach Denise and say, "OK, I think I might want in on this business...what's the deal?" She signed up soon after, and in less than two years, she promoted her way to the top of the company and is now making more in a month than she did in a year at her former job. Because Denise didn't force the interaction the first time around, Nikki felt comfortable approaching Denise when she was ready to get started...clearly she was worth the wait!

If you have ever been in sales, you know your success really just depends on the total number of people you reach with your product. For every yes you get, there are several no's that precede and follow—and that's just how it works! The sooner you become comfortable hearing no, the sooner you can move past it and find your next yes. One of our teammates, Debbie, was at an expo one weekend with her booth of products. She was asking the crowds walking by if they wanted to give her product a try, and one woman among many stopped in her tracks, disgusted, to say "no." Debbie shrugged her shoulders and said to her teammate, "I guess she doesn't like mustard..." and kept on going. If someone says no to you or your product, you have to remember that it really has nothing to do with you—some people will want your product and some people will not. There is nothing you can do to make certain people want your product; you can't sell steak to a vegetarian, but you have to keep asking to find out who the vegetarians are.

The only way you will really become comfortable with something you fear is by taking action and facing it head-on. The next couple of chapters are going to ask a lot of you because there is a lot to be done in the first three months of building your business. It will push your limits and ask you to step outside your comfort zone, but I promise you won't regret it if you can make the commitment. I'm not saying it will be easy, but I am saying it will be worth it.

Whenever people are having a tough time getting started, I like to give them the advice of one of my mentors, which is, "Get over yourself!" You can always find reasons or excuses to justify why you aren't doing something you know you should be, but at the end of the day, you are only hurting yourself and your chances for success. When you can "get over yourself" and move past all your doubts, insecurities and fears to get out there and give it a shot—you will be amazed at how much you can achieve.

In the first month, you should focus on building your foundation by following these steps to success—

Put yourself out there.

Order business cards (or whatever marketing tools your company has) with your contact information and website info as soon as you can and keep them on hand wherever you go. You should also establish yourself online right away to get your name and business out there in the open. With the growing popularity of social media and social networking sites today, you never know who's watching what you post—you could be attracting customers without even knowing it, so it's important to start branding yourself and your business online from the get-go.

Become a product of the product.

Do your homework by learning the ins and outs of your company's products, policies, tools and resources. What kind of people identify with your product? How does it compare to similar products on the market? What are the different ways you can market and sell your product?

Your First 30 Days

Because the beginning of any new adventure naturally creates a sense of excitement, it's critical that you capitalize on this initial excitement and energy to build a solid foundation for your business.

Think outside of the box to come up with new ways to share your product or service. The marketing tools that have been laid out for you by your company are great resources, but you will also want to explore other options, especially as time goes on and your go-to resources dry up temporarily. Maybe your company's specialty is a health product, so you might find some health-conscious people who are interested in your business or product at your gym, at the chiropractor's office, or the local health store.

This is just one example, but you have to think about the audience that your particular product appeals to, and how you might approach that audience in your local area (as well as online) to ensure that you always have new leads coming in.

On a more basic level, you'll want to read all of the training materials available, listen to all the calls you can, watch every webinar possible, and attend every event in your area. When you immerse yourself with the product you're promoting and learn about every aspect of your business opportunity, it makes selling your product a lot easier and a lot more fun— you grow your belief in the industry and your confidence in yourself at the same time. Not only that, but being knowledgeable and passionate about your business and the products you're selling allows the consumer to see your confidence and excitement and take it as a sign to trust you. When they can see that you genuinely believe in the quality of your products, it makes it easier for them to believe too. Your company's products may draw a lot of people in, but you also want those people to join your team—make sure you're always showcasing the business opportunity in addition to the products.

If you can't get excited about the products your company offers, you probably aren't in the right company! But if you do love the products you're selling, you and your family should be using them every day. The more you use it, the more you'll learn about it, and the more testimonials you'll collect—when you have real stories to tell people about your products, it resonates with them much more than the same corporate script they hear from everyone else. A personal testimony might take a little more work on your end, but it is so worth it— your customers will feel your passion for the products if you have your own story to tell.

Wearing apparel with your company's logo on it is also a great way to break the ice with someone and get talking about your business. Like I always say, you can't just talk about it; you have to be about it!

Create a long list of potential prospects.

And by long, we mean at least 100. Everyone who joins a network marketing company can go to their family and friends and get a couple people to buy products or sign up, but no one can sustain a network marketing business on family and friends alone. Creating a list of 100 people you can contact and share your product with forces you to step outside your comfort zone and talk to people beyond your immediate circle. Once you've listed all your close acquaintances, think about all the other groups, organizations, teams, and programs you're a part of. Your dentist's office, doctor's office, your children's teachers or sports teams, your church group, and any other person that you've connected with or been referred to is fair game!

Some people say, "there's no way I can come up with 100 names of people who would be interested in joining this business." I respond by asking, what if I gave you $1000 for every name you come up with? ...And that generally gets them to sit down and start writing. I say $1000 because once our business really started growing and our monthly paychecks hit five figures, I realized how truly valuable each and every distributor in my organization was.

The other thing I always tell new business owners is that you can't pre-judge anyone in this business—they only say they can't come up with 100 names because they can't think of 100 people who would they think would actually join, but you can never say no for someone else. In my experience, it's the people who you think will sign up who don't, and the people you think never would are the ones who join and become amazing leaders. When it comes to recruiting, it's one of the few situations where you can't trust your gut— everyone is a potential customer or business partner!

It might frighten you to approach these people that you don't know very well when you're first getting started, but you have to remember that the worst thing that can happen is a "no." It might sting to get a no from someone you know or trust, but it's better than constantly wondering what he or she might have said.

When you do finish your list of 100 names, enter all of them into a spreadsheet or another program that will help you keep them organized. You'll want to make note of all the information you have about them now (name, email, phone number), and also a note of the information you gather afterward (the dates you've contacted them, whether they said yes, no, or something in between, and any other notes that may be important to remember in the future). And because social media/social networking sites have become so popular in the last couple years, it's really smart to connect with each of your prospects on Facebook as well so you can begin cultivating those relationships that are so important to this business.

Exercise: Stop right now and text, email or Facebook message 10 people saying, "Have you heard of or tried _____?" (whatever your signature product is). When they respond yes or no, it opens the door for you to tell them more about it.

Plug-in to your community.

When you spend time with other people who are passionate and excited about the same things you are, the energy can be extremely contagious and advantageous to your business. If people see how excited you are about the products you sell, they will be more excited to learn about your products and what you do.

Not only that, but your upline and teammates are the perfect people to go when you're sad, frustrated or excited beyond belief with this business—they've experienced everything you're going through and they want to help you. When you're successful, they're successful.

Before Denise and I really nailed down our system for success, we had a few teammates who wanted to step up and take more responsibility before we knew exactly how to give them that extra responsibility. It was early on in our careers and we were still trying to discover a duplicable system for our new teammates. When Anna (who is now one of our leaders), joined our team, she was ready to go all-in from the get go. Anna's home was facing foreclosure and she knew that she had to take drastic measures with her new business if she wanted to save her house in time. Instead of getting discouraged that there wasn't an established system ready for her to follow, Anna instead said, "I'll just follow you guys around for a few days and do what you do." And that's exactly what she did— she shadowed us until she learned the ropes, and then she went out and did what we did on her own. I am so happy to share that Anna did save her house and is now making five figures a month.

One of my favorite passages from the Bible comes from Proverbs and touches on this subject—"He that walketh with wise men shall be wise: but a companion of fools shall be destroyed." Whenever someone asks me how they can get to the top of their business or industry, I say, talk to the people at the top! Spend time with them, ask questions, soak up their wisdom and do what they do. You don't have to reinvent the wheel when there are successful people all around you.

Whether you're hanging out with those people physically one-on-one, at a team training or event, or just on Facebook through a team group that you created, it is so important that you connect with your team. Sideline and upline relationships are very powerful in this business! We've got to get rid of that mentality that we're all in competition with one another and start thinking of ourselves as being in business together—there is a common goal that we're all working towards, why wouldn't we support and encourage each other to achieve what we're all working for?

Pitch your presentation and plan a launch party.

> Knowledge is power—the more you know about your products, company and presentation, the better off you'll be. If you don't know where to start, ask your teammates for help! Plug into others, shadow people, watch videos online, and role play with trusted friends or family. It doesn't matter if you're doing it well right now or not, what matters is that you're out there doing it! Don't forget the power of on-the-job training— you just have to get started and learn as you go.

Most companies have a system for duplication. Invest in your business and yourself by tagging along with teammates who know what they're doing whenever you get a chance. A lot of what stops us from being successful is fear, so get out there and build up your confidence by watching people on the spot—don't worry, you can hide behind someone else until you're ready. You'll be so surprised by how much you learn by watching someone else. You're never too old or too experienced to learn something new. Find your tool's system for success and try it. I've always believed that there's no better way to get started than to jump in both feet first!

You can give yourself a couple days to practice your presentation and get a feel for it, but don't spend too much time worrying about the exact wording because that will only stall your efforts—these first 30 days are all about stepping outside your comfort zone, so don't let yourself spend too long on any one task. If you let yourself avoid something you know needs to be done to be successful, you're only pushing your dreams further away.

Once you feel confident about your knowledge of the company, its products, and your presentation, pick a date within the first month (the sooner the better!) of launching your business to host your first party or event. If you really want to get on the fast track, do a double launch or launch your first party within your first 2 weeks. Remember, we're not planning a wedding here—like Nike says, just do it!

Choose an appropriate number of people from your list to invite to your home to listen in on your business opportunity so they can learn more about the products or services that you can offer them through your company. Quantity doesn't mean quality—rather than getting discouraged by a low number of people, focus on those people and how your products or business opportunity can help them. Pay close attention to them, answer their questions, and put all your efforts into serving them and their needs.

Most network marketing companies also have incentives setup for newbies when they're just getting started, so make sure you're hitting the recommended number of sales/sign- ups each month to earn those extra beginner bonuses.

And while we definitely encourage you to do your homework and attend trainings to get as familiarized as you can with your product and company, we don't want you to confuse spending hours and hours behind books or your computer screen with taking action. You learn best by doing, so you should learn enough to give a presentation, practice it a few times, and get out there and try it out! You won't become totally comfortable with it until you start doing it.

If you manage to complete all of these tasks in your first 30 days, you're going to be much further ahead in your business than most people ever get...so give yourself a pat on the back! Building a successful network marketing business requires you to wake up every day with the big picture in mind and the discipline to make it happen. It takes focus, organization, consistency, and hard work, but you are off to a great start! Remember, successful people are finishers. Don't let yourself think "if this works" but "when this works."

In the next chapter, we'll talk about what it takes to maintain your business once that initial excitement wears off, and how you can measure your progress along the way. In other words, we'll give you a test to let you know how well your business is coming along, and we'll also give you more valuable exercises/tips to keep your business going strong far past your first 30 days. Don't stop now... things are just getting good!

five.

WHAT CAN I DO TO KEEP THE MOMENTUM GOING?

"Nothing in this world can take the place of persistence. Talent will not; nothing is more common than unsuccessful people with talent. Genius will not; unrewarded genius is almost a proverb. Education will not; the world is full of educated failures. Persistence and determination alone are omnipotent."

—*Calvin Coolidge*

written by **DENISE WALSH**

You know what you want out of this business and have already begun working toward it, but it's going to take this type of continued commitment on a long-term basis before you really start experiencing the full freedom this industry can provide. In the meantime, however, you should start seeing small commission checks and bonuses within the next few months if you're following your company's "system for success. "

I know it can be discouraging when you consistently work at your business and your checks remain small for several months in a row—but I can assure you wholeheartedly that if you keep working your tail off, it will pay off. If you talk to anyone who's ever been really successful in network marketing, they will tell you how quickly your paychecks can make incredible jumps in a single month once you start gaining momentum. This chapter is going to help you gauge your progress thus far and outline your priorities for the next couple months going forward.

It's time to dive into the specific personal goals we believe you should strive to attain during the second and third months of launching your business. As Kami mentioned in the last chapter, laying a solid foundation for your business now will reward you for a lifetime.

The Next 30 Days

Remember that spreadsheet of contacts you created in the first few days of signing up and launching your business? I hope so! If you haven't been updating your spreadsheet with follow-up statuses and contacting new people regularly, it's time to add that task to your regular schedule. Talking with potential prospects should be something you do every day— whether it's people from your original list, posts on social media sites, strangers at the supermarket, or the teachers at your kid's school, you should be sharing your story whenever you get the chance.

Of course you don't want to be obnoxious, but there are easy and subtle ways to bring up your business in casual conversation all the time. Even a simple, "How are you?" or "What have you been up to?" can easily turn into "I'm great! I've recently become an entrepreneur and I'm having a lot of fun building my own business. How are you doing?" Or "I've actually been really busy scheduling parties for this new product I'm selling... what have you been up to?" By saying just enough, you pique their curiosity and make them want to learn more without having to force anything unnatural. When you can prompt them to ask questions first rather than "throwing up" information before they get a chance to ask, the conversation will flow much more naturally and easily.

If you still have names of people you haven't talked to from your list and you've only had one party or event so far, you should really strive to book at least one party or event per week until you develop a few solid teammates who are ready to get to work and start hosting parties themselves. You will feel more and more comfortable as you keep doing them, you'll increase your chances of finding new customers, and you'll be spreading the word of your business to a lot of people in a short amount of time.

Once you do run out of "warm" personal prospects to contact (people who you're already acquainted with), you'll have to start experimenting with the other ways you can market your product and find new customers. Spend time with the leaders in your company to find out which strategies your teammates have found success with. Your upline and teammates truly want to help you succeed, so don't be afraid to go to them when you need tips, advice, or a little extra encouragement to keep moving forward. They've been through what you're going through, so there's no need to do it alone.

If you're still feeling unsure about the direction of your business despite talking to your teammates for help, I really recommend spending some more time familiarizing yourself with the industry itself, and how your company operates within this industry. If you feel ill equipped to answer questions from potential prospects or don't completely believe in the product or the opportunity you're selling, it's hardly surprising that you would have trouble signing up other teammates.

When I first started working my direct sales business, I made the same mistake in those first few months—I was afraid to own my new business as a legitimate career path. I struggled to believe that it was really a viable way of making money. I didn't totally understand the industry, so instead of being a proud entrepreneur, I was a clinical psychologist...who also did network marketing. I tried building my business with this mentality for a few months, but as I kept working at it, I continued learning. I read all the books on business, leadership, networking, and relationship building that I could get my hands on—I listened to the team calls from the leaders in the company, re-watched the webinars, and started attending more team events. Once I began to better understand how the system worked and how I could use my unique talents within that system, I started believing that I too could be successful if I duplicated that system.

I know there's been a lot of information thrown at you in the last several pages, so here's a recap of your action plan for the first 60 days—

Order your marketing materials with your contact information as well as some apparel with your company's logo on it.

Why this is important—*Your marketing materials should be taken with you everywhere you go so you can leave someone with your information when they want to learn more about what you're doing and your company clothing will be a great conversation starter/ice breaker when you wear it out in public.*

Immerse yourself with information about your company, your business opportunity, and your products.

Why this is important—*Knowledge is power. The more you know about your business, the more confident you will be talking about it, and the easier it will be for you to answer any questions that arise. (But once again— you learn best by DOING, so don't spend more than 2-3 days training yourself at home.)*

Introduce your involvement with your new business online.

Why this is important—*Sharing your business on your social media profiles (Facebook, Twitter, Google+, etc.) is like FREE advertising. You never know who is seeing your posts and considering your products/opportunity.*

Create a list of "out of the box" marketing strategies.

Why this is important—*It's likely that whatever company you promote has some marketing strategies laid out for you (home parties, coupons, etc.), but eventually you will want to explore some other ways to market your business to reach new people. Having a list that you can refer back to at any time will save you the stress of trying to brainstorm creative ideas when you really need them.*

Explore your product line by trying/using as many as you can right away!

Why this is important—*When you have personal testimonials/stories about the products you're selling, people will be much more willing to listen and try them for themselves than the person who uses the same old script for every product.*

Create a list of 100 potential customers.

Why this is important—*Sales is a numbers game and people you know are generally more likely to try your product without too much convincing because they already know and trust you to some extent. When you're first getting started, it's smart to approach your "warm market" first while you're still learning the ropes and perfecting your approach.*

Text/email/message 10 of those people immediately.

Why this is important—*Texting/online messaging has become such a regular part of communication today that there's no reason you can't start contacting people right away. You don't have to say much—you can just ask if they've heard of your product or tried it, and when they respond yes or no, that opens up the door for you to tell them more.*

Plug-in to your community.

Why this is important—*There is so much you can learn from your teammates, old and new. They are also a huge source of support for you and your dreams, and you will definitely need that extra support at times—plug-in to your community and connect with your teammates... you won't regret it.*

Practice your presentation and shadow successful people on your team.

Why this is important—*Practicing your presentation in advance will make you feel and appear more confident to the people you're presenting to. Shadowing people who are already successful will give you a good idea of what you should be focusing your time on and how you can be successful by doing that too.*

Launch (or re-launch) your first party or event.

Why this is important—*If you're not getting your products in people's hands and telling them about your opportunity, you will never find people to join your team. You have to be intentional about sharing your business with others.*

Follow-up, follow-up and follow-up some more.

Why this is important—*I think most everyone who has worked in this industry is guilty of not following-up with people as much as they should have at some point in their career. Just because someone says "no" right now, doesn't mean it's a no forever. Unless someone clearly tells you "I'm not interested and I never will be," it's fair game to follow-up with them every couple months to see if their circumstances have changed.*

The Final 30 Days

The final 30 days of your first three months is when you should make a mental note to tie up any loose ends with another round of follow-ups. Anyone who has tried your product, bought your product, or signed up to sell your product should be contacted. If they tried it, ask if they're interested in purchasing that product; if they bought it, ask if they're happy with their results; if they signed up to sell it, you should already know how they're doing!

When you're finished, update your spreadsheet/list yet again to reflect the follow-ups you've just made.

On top of taking care of these follow-ups, it's also a good idea to send thank-you cards to all of the people who took the time to meet with you, regardless of whether or not they became a customer/distributor. Throughout this business, it's likely that you will experience some rejection from the people you want to get through to most—that rejection is difficult to swallow, but it's also an inevitable part of the business that you have to get past in order to succeed. That being said, one of the most powerful things you can do is show gratitude to the people who did take the time to listen. At the end of the day, it's a numbers game in a people business—treat people with respect and you will be rewarded for it.

Now that you're reaching the end of your first 90 days of building your business, you're probably wondering how you can measure your progress when you aren't making much (if any) money yet. And if you aren't making any money yet, don't be discouraged! You have just begun planting the seeds of your business; it may take a while for those seeds to bloom into beautiful flowers, but if you continue to take proper care of those seeds day in and day out, they will transform and be worth every minute you've waited.

If you've been following along with the exercises and suggestions we've made for you thus far, you are in great shape! But for those who like to make a mental checklist, we've come up with a series of questions to ask yourself about the work you've done in these first 90 days.

☐ *How much do I know about my company?*

☐ *Can I explain the opportunity and its compensation plan to a prospect with little to no difficulty?*

☐ *Am I knowledgeable about the product line and any specific interest groups of people it may appeal to?*

☐ *Am I comfortable with my presentation? Am I attending as many trainings and events as I can?*

☐ *Am I plugging into my community and connecting with my team?*

☐ *Am I talking to new people every day?*

☐ *Do I feel defeated when someone says no to me?*

☐ *Am I exploring multiple ways to market my product?*

☐ *How many people have told me to connect with them again at a later time?*

☐ *Have I followed up with everyone I need to?*

☐ *Am I scheduling parties or recruiting people to host parties every month?*

☐ *Am I working as hard as I possibly can to start my business off on the right track?*

Because it's still early on in your journey, you can't expect to know the answer behind every question you get asked. I've been with my company for almost 7 years, and I still get asked questions that I have to find out the answer to or double-check myself on. You can never know it all, but you should feel pretty comfortable with your knowledge behind the products, company and opportunity by the end of your 2nd month. Getting active within your community and making an effort to go to the events and meeting new people is a really important aspect of this business, so if you're not already doing this... make it a higher priority! You can't just be a fly on the wall in this industry—you need to network, socialize, and build relationships within your team and outside of it whenever you have the opportunity.

A fun little test you can give yourself is the "30 second elevator pitch." If you walked into an elevator and saw an old friend or acquaintance who asked about your work, could you give them a 30-second pitch on your business that would get them interested enough to ask more about it? Would you be able to answer their basic questions confidently and easily? If yes, this can be your go-to speech from now on whenever you strike up a conversation with a stranger and you know you have a limited time to talk (e.g. standing in line at the grocery story, sitting in the waiting room at the dentist's office, etc.). If you haven't nailed it down yet, keep practicing your elevator pitch until you can confidently give an exciting overview of your business in a minute or less. You'll be surprised by how many opportunities you get to strike up a friendly conversation with a stranger when you're intentional about looking for those instances.

And now that you have been talking to more and more people (we hope!) about your business, that most likely means there are also more people who you need to keep following up with. A lot of times people will say, "it's been 3 months since I heard from him/her, I don't think they're interested" because they don't believe that someone will really turn around and change their mind a few months down the road. Don't make this mistake and assume a no for anyone until they've made it blatantly clear that they don't want you to contact them again. Everyone is a different kind of customer with different appeals, but most people do need to see/hear about a product several times before they will even consider trying it. Keep that in mind when you're debating following-up with someone or making another post on Facebook—don't be obnoxious and attack people with your posts or phone calls, but continue reminding them until they tell you otherwise.

Checklist aside, if you know you're working as hard as you possibly can, and continue to do so for the foreseeable future, you will be one of the few people in this world who knows what it's like to live a life of total freedom. Network marketing is a unique opportunity for anyone because it's one of the few business models that doesn't require a certain "type" of person. You don't need a formal education, you don't need much money to get started, and you don't even need to have prior experience in sales. The beauty of this business lies in persistence—if you work longer and harder than 90% of people who get involved in network marketing, you will retire faster and with more security than 90% of people.

Persistence, however, is an action that goes hand in hand with self-discipline—you can't be persistently consistent if you don't have the self-discipline necessary to stay on track. Life is full of temptations and it's even more difficult to resist them as an entrepreneur who works from home and chooses their own schedule. Can you skip watching the premiere of your favorite TV show to work a couple extra hours instead? Are you willing to turn down a night out with friends to do some last-minute work before your paycheck is submitted? Self-discipline is a skill that you need to develop (if you haven't already), and the next chapter will cover why it plays such an important role in this business and how you can start strengthening your ability to get down to business and stay there.

HOW CAN I GET MORE WORK DONE?

"Talent is cheaper than table salt. What separates the talented individual from the successful one is a lot of hard work."

— *Stephen King*

written by **KAMI DEMPSEY**

Self-discipline is the single most important attribute an entrepreneur can have. We don't have bosses telling us when to get to work or when to finish a project, so it is entirely up to us to decide what needs to be done, how it needs to be done, and how soon it needs to be completed. Because I was an athlete and coach for many years, self-discipline is a skill that I learned at a very young age. As I've gotten older and had to implement more self- discipline in my every day efforts, I can clearly see how a lack of this skill can severely affect an entrepreneur's success—when you don't learn to control your time, your time controls you.

This chapter is going to give you the insight you need to know just how much your self- discipline (or lack thereof) can impact your business (I'll give you a hint—strong self- discipline produces some crazy miracles that I can't wait to tell you about). Not only that, but I'm also going to let you in on some awesome time managements tactics that will let you get more work done in less time so you can spend your days working smarter...not harder.

Self-Made Success

I've only been in network marketing for six years now, but within that time, I have witnessed some amazing, life-changing, holy-cow-I-can't-believe-that-just-happened stuff. I've seen the light bulb go on in people's heads when they hear about the opportunity, and then watched them run with it, full-speed, until they've literally turned their lives around. I've seen families whose homes were facing foreclosure turn their finances around in a matter of a few months. I've seen countless women start building a business for some extra "fun money" and wound up replacing their husband's income.

I love this industry because it brings in people from so many backgrounds, yet everyone has different reasons for getting involved. One couple I know were happily working as pastors for their church for several years—they enjoyed what they were doing, but didn't like that they had to completely rely on the church for their income. They heard about our company and started building their own business as a way to bring in some extra money on the side. Within a few years, they were both able to retire from their positions so they could stop relying solely on the church for money and spend more time volunteering. Another teammate of mine, Shelby, was a mother of one with another baby on the way while her husband was stationed in Afghanistan. She joined this business while she was pregnant with her second child and got to work right away knowing there would be big expenses ahead of her. Within a year and a half, Shelby was making five figures a month. And because Shelby made her family financially independent, the military sent her husband home since he would not be a burden on the economy. Shelby's self-discipline actually allowed her to retire her husband from Afghanistan!

These are just a few of the many, many miracles I've witnessed on our team alone, not to mention what goes on worldwide with network marketing. Needless to say, this industry has allowed a lot of people to make a lot of amazing achievements.

So, how do people manage to overcome lifelong habits and instantly change their futures forever? Self-discipline. While that answer might seem too simplistic to some, it's really what separates us as individuals—do you wish and hope for things to happen? Or do you make them happen? When our teachers and parents told us that we could be anything we wanted to when we were younger, they were only half right—you can be anything you want, if you have enough discipline to make it happen. Very few people are born with a raw, natural talent that leads them to a life of success. Even the people who are blessed with a natural gift still have to work at it to strengthen their skills and continue improving. Mozart, for example, is someone we think of when we hear the words, "natural talent." He started playing piano and creating beautiful works of art when he was just five years old. What people don't think about, is how often and intensively he continued practicing piano day after day, year after year, throughout his entire life. So even though it's clear that Mozart had a God-given gift to play piano, there is no way he would have become one of the greatest composers of all time if he didn't discipline himself to keep practicing and improving every day.

Some people have come to define self-discipline as doing what needs to be done, even when you don't feel like it. I like this definition because it hits on a very important point: it doesn't matter if you're tired, sick, sad, mad, or anything else—if you're disciplined, you do it anyway. No excuses are allowed. And because no excuses are permitted, self-discipline is a skill that lets people accomplish the (seemingly) impossible. It's what allows every day athletes to become Olympic medal-winning athletes, what allows mediocre musicians to become legends, and what allows some people to make their wildest dream a reality.

Too often people try to blame their problems and lack of success on someone else. While it's believable that you began your bad habits because of the poor influence of someone else, it's unacceptable to continue blaming someone else when you know better. Regardless of your childhood, your parents, your past relationships, your environment, the economy, or anything else that may affect you—you are responsible for your actions. How many times have you heard those radical rags to riches stories on the news? And how many of those people just "got lucky?" I'd say very few. Most of them got to where they are today because they got sick and tired of being sick and tired©—they made a decision to change the course of their life, and that's exactly what they did. They stopped making excuses and started taking action. Of course it's more difficult to accept responsibility than it is to point blame, but everything that's worthwhile in life is difficult at times. And how you overcome that difficulty (or don't) is what determines your character as a person—are you someone who throws in the towel when things get tough? Or do you keep trekking because you know that every step you take will put you closer to your goals?

Not-So-Instant Gratification

The real difference between people who are self-disciplined and those who are not is their ability to see and understand the link between their every day actions and the "big picture." Whatever it is that you want most out of life, you have to want it badly enough that you're willing to work toward it every day, knowing that the day you actually get what you want may be very far in the future. If you're someone who's very self-disciplined, you realize that every day is an opportunity to work toward that brighter future. Every action you take (or don't), is going to have an effect on the person you become and the future you have. Those who are not self-disciplined, on the other hand, make every decision based on how they feel in the moment. They are more likely to give up pre-determined plans if something else more fun comes up, and they are more likely to make excuses to rationalize their behavior. Those who are not self-disciplined have a very difficult time turning down situations where "instant gratification" is guaranteed.

Someone who suffers from a lack of discipline could be planning a nice, home-cooked meal that is healthy and delicious, but when their spouse offers to bring home pizza, they let their initial plans fall apart because pizza is the easier option. They might try to justify their decision to have pizza by telling themselves, "Oh, it's just this one time..." but they know better—if you allow yourself to break your word once, what's going to stop you from doing it again? When you're self-disciplined, you have the willpower to do what you say you're going to do, when you say you're going to do it, and you don't let any excuse stop you from getting it done. Even if you're not someone who grew up with strong self-discipline skills, it doesn't mean that you can't develop them now. It will take practice (like anything else), but it's a skill that will continue rewarding you for the rest of your life.

So, if you do want to start owning your time and making the most out of every minute (as most entrepreneurs do), you need to start setting specific goals, giving yourself deadlines, and fulfilling the promises you make to yourself. We all know it's important to have goals, yet many of us set ourselves up for failure when we set goals without any plan of action and don't write them down. When you set vague goals like, "I want to make more money" or "I want to lose weight," you're bound to be disappointed by the lack of results because you didn't give yourself a chance to succeed in the first place. If you're sick of being disappointed, tired of "almost" achieving your goals, and ready to make your aspirations your reality—goal setting combined with self-discipline is the answer.

Excuses Be Gone!

Now is the time to show yourself what you're made of! Self-discipline isn't just a secret skill that lets you accomplish more of your goals, it's also a natural way to boost your self- esteem and mood. When you're productive and crossing things off your to-do list, you feel good about yourself. When you turn down the pizza your husband offers to bring home and cook a healthy meal instead, you feel good. When you keep the promises you make to yourself, you set yourself up for a happier future, and that feels good too! But, in order to accomplish your goals, you need to know exactly what they are and how soon you want to accomplish them. Not only that, but you have to distinguish your short-term goals from your long-term goals and get in the habit of working toward both each and every day.

Time-Management Tactics

For short-term goals and every day errands, one of my favorite things to do is the "top three list." Every night before I go to bed, I write down three things that I absolutely want to get accomplished by the end of the next day. It almost seems too easy to write down just three things, but when the day begins and unexpected distractions consume your attention, your top three list will keep you on track. If there are five tasks you really need to get done, make it a top five list...the point is—when you write down your highest priority activities the night before, you can start your day with direction. You won't be wasting time thinking about what you need to do next or where you need to go; you'll be focusing on the job ahead, ready to cross it off your list as soon as it's done.

Another time management tactic that can be really beneficial is another kind of to-do list, but this one is a bit broader and puts more focus on your week as a whole. Because this list forces you to think about the week ahead, it's best to do it on Monday morning right when you wake up. (Mondays are only scary when you don't know what you're getting into!)

All you need to do is take out a blank sheet of paper and write down everything you can think of that you need to get done this week. You can always add to it, but you should brainstorm as many tasks as you can think of when you wake up. Once you're done, put a number 1 next to everything you want to get done by the end of the day. Put a number 2 next to everything you want to finish by the end of tomorrow, and a number 3 by everything you want to finish by the end of the week. Once you've numbered all your items, look at your number 1s and rank them with letters according to their importance. The most important, urgent task should be ranked "1A," the next, "1B" and so on. Do this with your number 2s and number 3s as well. When you've finished your list and you're ready to take on the day, make your "1A" task your absolute priority and don't let yourself get distracted until it's done. This way, even if you don't get any other task on your list done, you've already got the most important thing out of the way. Take out your list the following mornings and update/add anything that needs changes.

To-do lists are great to keep your every day errands and activities under control, but there are a few specific parameters you should keep in mind when you're setting up your short and long-term goals. For every goal you create, ask yourself the following questions—

- [ ] *Have I written my goal on paper?—Writing out your goal is extremely important! It only takes a minute, but communicating your goal on papers sends a message to your subconscious and holds you more accountable. When you just say you want to do something, it disappears into thin air when something more fun arises.*

- [ ] *Is my goal specific enough? —Did you write down something vague and difficult to gauge or is your goal clear and intentional? I want to lose weight vs. I want to lose 15 lbs.*

- [ ] *Is my goal measurable?—Will you be able to measure the progress of your success easily or is it too broad to evaluate? I want to lose 15 lbs. vs. I want to lose 15 lbs. in the next three months. Give yourself a realistic deadline to work with to make sure you are constantly working toward your goals.*

If your goals are written, specific and measurable, you are well on your way to success! In Brian Tracy's book, No Excuses!: The Power of Self Discipline, he says that only 3 percent of adults have written goals and plans, but this 3 percent earns more than all of the other 97 percent put together. If you're committed, your goals will be your future soon enough if you follow through with the necessary actions. Take your goals seriously and spend some time really thinking about what you want and what you can do to make it happen. There are no unrealistic goals. They're only unrealistic if you try to take them all on at once—take each goal and break it down into smaller, easier steps. It may take you longer to get there, but it's far better than staying in the same place. Benjamin Franklin once said, "He that is good for making excuses is seldom good for anything else." If you notice yourself starting to make excuses for anything that you've already committed to doing, discipline yourself to follow through with your word and get the job done.

It's going to take some time to develop your self-discipline skills, but the rewards of perfecting these skills will literally change your life forever. It's not just about money or success—it's about being the best person you can be and making every moment count. In order to do that, you also need to be confident in where you're headed and how you're getting there. Self-doubt is a feeling that sneaks up on every one of us at some point or another, but the next chapter will help you learn how you can cope with that doubt and turn it into confidence. When you have the confidence to take on challenges that you never thought you could, anything is possible.

seven.

WHAT STOPS MOST PEOPLE FROM BEING SUCCESSFUL IN THIS INDUSTRY?

"There is only one way to avoid criticism: do nothing, say nothing, and be nothing."

—*Aristotle*

*written by **DENISE WALSH***

Everyone is afraid of something. It appears to be a natural, instinctive feeling because we start developing fears at a very young age, but fears are learned. We learn to fear things because of past experiences, past failures, what we don't know, and what we don't understand. We say stuff like, "I don't know if I can," "I don't know how" or "I've never done that before." The trouble is, when you say these things too often, you begin to believe them and internalize them for the truth. This kind of self-fulfilling prophecy is a problem for countless individuals. They continue to fear what they don't know or understand, and soon, they start doubting their every move. This fear of failure prevents people from success more than any other factor. And chances are, you've let fear stop you from accomplishing something you've really wanted to do at least once, if not many times. But if you're ready to stop letting fear and self-doubt control your life, this chapter will guide you through your transformation.

Overcoming self-doubt is really one of the most difficult aspects of direct sales—I certainly struggled with it. Between the family and friends who will tell you network marketing is just "a pyramid scheme" and the strangers who will shake their head as soon as you say "direct sales," it's not always easy to overcome the naysayers' negativity. And while it's not an easy task to stay positive despite the discouraging comments from the people around you, it's crucial that you learn how to rise above it. After all, do you want to be the person sitting on the sidelines watching others do what you wish you could do? Or do you want to learn how you can conquer your fears, grow your confidence, get off the sidelines, and get into the game?

In order to take control of your fears and self-doubt, you must first understand what these feelings are stealing away from you. Not only does self-doubt fill your mind with ideas of inferiority, but it robs you of your self-worth, your ambition, and ultimately, your happiness. I mentioned earlier that when I first started working my business, I was afraid to own it. I doubted myself and my ability to sell my products, and I doubted the company I was involved in—this was a terrible way for me to think and feel when I had just launched my new business because those feelings were transparent to everyone I approached.

Instead of sensing the genuine passion I now have for my company's products and business plan, they sensed the fear and doubt in my words. I always told people I was a psychologist before I told them I was an entrepreneur, but the whole reason I started my own business was so I could quit my job as a psychologist! Looking back, it's no surprise that I had trouble finding teammates when I talked to people with such fear. Why would anyone want to join my team if I didn't have complete belief in the opportunity myself? I struggled to own my business as a "real business" because like so many others, I had pre-conceived notions about whether or not network marketing could really be a viable career path. I loved the idea of this lifestyle, but I wasn't totally "sold" on its legitimacy because I still doubted myself.

With my business off to a slow start, I asked Kami for some advice on how to overcome these feelings of uneasiness and doubt. Even though she was new to all of this too, Kami was always so confident and full of energy that I couldn't help but wonder what made our perspectives so different. Once I called her and we met to talk, I realized that Kami wasn't fearless after all—she doubted herself just like anyone else, but she found a way to think about her fears differently. Kami loved the relationship building aspect of this business— meeting new people and listening to their stories was easy, but she feared the follow-up process and coming off "too pushy" about the products.

So instead of focusing on the part she didn't like, she focused on the part she did: Kami made it her mission to talk to as many new people as she could, whenever she could, however she happened to meet them. Of course she still followed-up with her prospects, but she really focused most of her time on relationship building. When Kami poured her energy into what she loved, people could sense her passion right away. And when people sensed that sincerity when they spoke with her, they learned to trust her and ultimately, follow her. Not only that, but as Kami continued to do more and more follow-up, she realized that it was never a big deal to begin with—she only disliked it because it didn't come as naturally to her as the other aspects of the business.

This is true for many things we fear; we only fear them because we aren't familiar with them. More often than not, you're going to realize that you make problems out to be much bigger in your head than they are in reality. When you learn to confront your fears as soon as they arise, you train your brain to become less and less fearful of future unfamiliar activities. And if you continue to confront your fears face on, they will eventually disappear completely and turn into confidence!

After I talked to Kami and realized how much my doubts about "owning the business" were hurting my chances of being successful, I decided to put my energy into the aspects of my business that excited me. I've always been good at talking to new people and making them feel comfortable right away, so I really focused my efforts on being a "real friend" to every lead I talked to. Because so much of this industry relies on the relationships you create, my business started to thrive as soon as I put my unique skill-set to work. I treated my leads like real friends rather than just customers, and it worked better than I could have ever imagined. When I asked questions about their lives, families, and dreams, they asked about mine—and when people asked questions about my story, it opened the door for me to explain exactly what this business means to me, my family and our future. When I shared that personal information about myself and my family, people were more likely to ask more questions about the business without me forcing it. If my prospect continued showing interest once I got into more details about the business opportunity, it gave me an opening to invite them to join my team. I made sure they knew that they would have my full support if they joined my team, and I'd be there for them every step along the way. Because we had already developed somewhat of a relationship by talking as friends first, they were always more willing and excited to learn more about the business side of things when the subject arose naturally.

I couldn't believe what a difference it made to focus on what I did well—not only was I signing up more people than I ever did before, but my confidence was growing a little more with every phone call. When I found what I was good at and put my energy into that, my doubts about the business faded away. I was only scared of "owning" the business because I doubted my own abilities to be successful—when I put my abilities to work without worrying about whether or not I'd be successful, I was successful without even trying.

I know it's easier to hide from your fears and hope that they'll go away on their own, but you'll never solve any problems by running away from them. Being courageous takes discipline, but you'll never regret being brave—you only regret the things you wish you would have done. It's easier to say "go face your fears!" than it is to actually get out there and confront them, but it's a necessary obstacle to cross if you want to reach your full potential for success. You can't be everything you are destined to be if you have doubts in your mind or fear in your heart.

If you have already started working in this industry, you know rejection is inevitable—the key is learning not to take this rejection personally...ever. It will never benefit you to take someone saying "no" to you as a reflection of how they think of you as a person. When you eliminate your fear of failure and rejection and focus all of your energy on winning, you will no longer have an option to fail.

Ask yourself what are the worst things that could possibly happen with this business—you could lose the money you invested in it if you quit, people could turn you down, and some people might even say mean things about the company you represent or the products you sell. Sure, some of these things are unpleasant...but are any of them unbearable? Will any of them ruin your life? Probably not.

Now let's look at the other end of the spectrum. What are the best possible things that can happen with this business—you could build some amazing new relationships, you could find total financial freedom, and you could change your and your family's life forever, leaving a legacy of wealth and freedom behind. Looking at the worst-case and best-case scenarios, do you think it's worth trying? I can't even imagine what my life would look like today if I didn't give myself a chance—I hope you give yourself a chance to live the life of your dreams too.

If you do decide that you're worth the investment (you are!) and want to keep learning what you can do to grow your business, the next chapter will help you identify what you do best, and allow you to spend more time exercising those strengths for even greater results!

eight.

WHAT IF I DON'T HAVE ANY UNIQUE TALENTS?

"We are each gifted in a unique and important way. It is our privilege and our adventure to discover our own special light."

—Mary Dunbar

written by **DENISE WALSH**

Imagine a team of committed, motivated people who are all working toward the same goal, but each individual is free to work in a way that exercises their natural strengths and talents. What is the result? A group of people who are happy to work their hardest, and an organization that runs smoothly and efficiently because no one is wasting time or distracting themselves from a job they don't care about.

Now, what is the reality of most organizations and businesses today? Employees are hired under the assumption that they can be trained enough in any area to qualify for any entry- level position and work their way up. What is the result? A group of bored and unhappy people who waste as much time as they can manage because they are not interested in working on the tasks assigned to them, and an organization that wastes money and resources training people to do mediocre work at jobs they don't care about. It's extremely inefficient, yet it's the norm in most workplaces today.

If you're unhappy with the way your team operates and the results you're producing, this chapter will show you what you can do to start producing better work from happier teammates in less than a month.

Our culture has come to embrace the idea that a person's greatest weakness is their greatest area for improvement. While it's true that almost any skill can be learned with enough discipline and commitment, it doesn't mean we should focus all of our discipline and time on the skills we don't have. Instead we should focus our time, energy and resources into identifying our pre-existing strengths, and what we can do to achieve further excellence in those areas.

From there, we can go on to identify the individual and unique talents of each of our teammates. It may take more time initially to identify the individual strengths of each and every teammate rather than assuming everyone can learn a particular skill, but the benefits of this business model provide much greater rewards. And, applying this principle to the business model of network marketing makes even more sense. In direct sales, every team needs a great leader to instill the vision of freedom and possibility into the minds of their teammates. If this leader can help show each individual the potential of their dreams and how to use their individual strengths to create personal and team success, the results can be life-changing.

As a young girl, I always wanted to help other people in need— whether it was family members who needed to be taken care of when they were sick, friends or siblings who needed advice, or a stranger that seemed sad and in need of someone to cheer them up, I was always willing to stick my hand out and help. This passion for others led me to become a clinical psychologist after college, but like I mentioned before, I ultimately found that the politics and paperwork of my position outweighed the time I was able to spend with those who genuinely wanted my help. I like to think that I provided meaningful guidance to the clients I once had, but I now see that my greatest strengths come alive when I am encouraging others to discover theirs.

Once I really became engaged in building my own business, I knew that my true calling was in this position of leadership. I feel so energized and excited every time I get the opportunity to instill confidence and courage into someone who wants to follow their dreams. My teammates often thank me for believing in them before they believed in themselves. But the truth is, most of the time I just want to thank them—they have no idea how rewarding it is to watch someone overcome their biggest doubts in themselves and go on to achieve things they never thought they were capable of. I thank God every day that I found my purpose and calling in this business.

Realize Your God-Given Talents

Whether we like to admit it or know it, every one of us is born with some form of natural talent. It may not fit into the narrow categories of skills that we generally think of when we think of natural talents (natural athletes, musicians, public speakers, artists, etc.), but that doesn't make it any less important or valuable. In fact, those individuals who have talents that don't fit into these common categories are generally more valuable because less people have them. It's also possible that you have strong skills in a particular area, but if you don't have a passion for those activities, they are not your greatest strengths—if you don't enjoy it, you won't produce the most quality work you're capable of producing. A skill may be an area where you're capable of performing above average work, but a strength is an area where you consistently perform excellent work and enjoy doing so.

Once you can identify your own personal strengths and put them to work, you'll be happier to do the work that's necessary, you will produce stronger results and be far more productive, and your business will be more successful. Not only that, but once you become a greater judge of your own strengths, it will put you in a better position to point out the unique gifts of the people around you. When you can help show others in your organization where their strengths lie, your business will run far more efficiently—people will be working on jobs that suit their individual strengths vs. being assigned to random tasks purely because they can be trained to do it.

If you don't already know what your strengths are (don't worry, many people don't!), there are some different activities you can do to help you recognize your God-given gifts.

Make a list of everything you consider yourself to be above average at. Consider all areas of your life, not just what you do at your job. Even if it's something that you think might be an insignificant skill (good at making small talk, very quick typist, love taking pictures, etc.), you never know where it might be valuable in your business.

Challenge yourself to come up with *at least* 10 things you excel at. Once you've finished your list, look it over and ask yourself these questions about each skill you listed.

☐ **Does time fly when I'm using/exercising this skill?**

☐ **Is this a skill that I look forward to using?**

☐ **Does using this skill make me feel energized and excited?**

☐ **Does this skill come easily to me?**

☐ **Would I enjoy my job more if I got to use this skill on a regular basis?**

If you answered 'yes' to three or more of these questions for any given skill you listed, congratulations, you can put a star next to that skill as it is likely one of your strengths. Once you've identified one or more skill that may be a strength of yours, put it to the test! Intentionally use each of the skills you listed over the next few weeks and then ask yourself the questions above again. Do your answers remain true when you use this skill regularly and intentionally? If so, these are the strengths you should keep working on to improve yourself, your self-esteem, and your business.

Marcus Buckingham, the author of *Now, Discover Your Strengths* advises readers to write down the activities you engage in on a daily basis and make a note of whether they energize you or drain you. As he says, "A better definition of strength is an activity that makes you feel strong. And a weakness is an activity that makes you feel weak. Even if you're good at it, if it drains you, it's a weakness." Keep in mind, however, that there can be a good and a bad feeling of "being drained"—is it a feeling of exhausted accomplishment after tough, but fulfilling work? Or is it mentally and/or physically draining without a reward?

Once you've successfully identified at least one of your strengths, it's time to take action and use your unique skill set to your advantage. Think about your strength(s) in relationship to your specific business—where can your put your strengths in motion to propel your business forward? Maybe you're a great writer who can write amazing blog posts that promote your business. Or maybe you're an extremely organized person who can help their teammates fit more parties and events into their schedules to benefit the whole team's success.

Are there any necessary strengths you're missing personally that another teammate may have? Once you've identified the areas of your business that your strength can be applied to and the areas of weakness where you need the help of your teammates, you can start taking action and experiencing the rewards of your work. It may take some time to get an effective and smooth working system in place, but there is no doubt that better work will be produced. When a group of people is motivated to achieve their goals and each individual knows how to use their unique strengths to accomplish them, success is inevitable! Not many people know what their strengths are and how/when to use them, but many of the people who do are leaders.

Leaders are extremely important in any organization, but especially significant in network marketing—the next chapter will explain why that is and what you can do to become a better leader toward your own team.

nine.

HOW DO I BECOME A BETTER LEADER?

"If your actions inspire others to dream more, learn more, do more and become more, you are a leader."

—John Quincy Adams

written by **KAMI DEMPSEY**

What Makes a Great Leader?

Leaders are doers. They have a vision for themselves and their organization, and they go to great lengths to see that vision become a reality. When there are obstacles, problems, negativity, and quitters who get in the way of this vision, the leader rises to the occasion, finds a solution, and gets back to work. They don't expect anyone to do something that they wouldn't be willing to do themselves. Leadership has nothing to do with the title and everything to do with influence. As my mentor and friend Bob Goshen puts it, leadership is the positive, progressive influence on others.

Most of all, a true leader is a servant leader—they find purpose in their position when they can help others live life at their greatest potential. They love instilling confidence into those who follow them and creating a sense of a community within their teams. Great leaders leave the world a better place than they found it in because they are incessantly improving themselves and the people around them. Leaders have this special ability to help their teammates improve because they can identify the individual strengths of each person. When you have a strong leader in every one of your teams who can inspire and motivate each person to work at their highest potential, the results are truly astounding. If you want to learn more about how you can become an inspiring leader for your own team, you're in the right place.

While I could go on and on talking about what it means to be a good leader, I think it's more important to talk about what a great leader does and how you can work toward developing these qualities in your own life. Becoming a leader will require you to take on more responsibility and risk in your business, but the rewards are truly amazing and life changing. One of my favorite quotes on this topic comes from Pat Pearson—"Instead of focusing on yourself and how you feel, be totally focused on the person in front of you, on her hopes and dreams, and how you can share with her a way to achieve them. Sharing a gift of a better life is the most wonderful thing you can do!"

So What Do Great Leaders Do?

1 *Great leaders solve problems*—A big distinction that you can draw between leaders and regular business owners is the way they handle problems. Leaders respond to problems by focusing on the solution while business owners react to the problem itself. About a year ago our company had a shortage of our best-selling product for over a month and a lot of people panicked. Business owners worried that their paychecks would plummet and they'd lose out on a lot of customers. Fortunately the leaders in our company turned the situation around completely— they told their teammates that having a shortage of this product meant the company was experiencing massive growth; it wasn't something to worry about, but rather something to be excited about because it meant even more sales as soon as the product was back in stock. If the leaders in our company hadn't responded to the problem in a way that calmed their teammates' fears, it could have caused total pandemonium within our organization.

Exercise: Think back to any recent problems regarding your business and ask yourself how you reacted: Did you react like a nervous newbie or response like a calm and collected leader? If you reacted in a panicked manner, what could have you have done differently to respond like a leader?

Looking forward, allow yourself some extra time to handle problems that arise to ensure that you have a chance to think about the different ways you can solve that problem. Are you getting caught up in the issue itself or are you focusing all of your energy on the solution? Stay clear-headed and tell yourself, "I am a leader. I will handle this like a leader." Practice this exercise until you have developed a habit to problem solve with a clear-mind and calm actions.

Once you've mastered your problem-solving skills, you must also make sure you have accountability with someone you trust—before you say or respond to any problems, talk to your accountability partner to ensure that what you're thinking is actually what you want to share with the group. When you're in a position of leadership, you cannot take back your words or actions after you realize they weren't received well. We've all seen countless news stories of politicians or professionals slipping up on air, saying something they shouldn't have once they "go off" on a topic, and then coming back to apologize the next day because they "didn't mean" to say what they said. You can't afford to make these kinds of mistakes, so an accountability partner or council of leaders who you can trust is really important to maintain your positive image.

2 *Great leaders use their time wisely*—The difference between good time management and bad time management is often the difference between great success and mediocrity. Leaders know how to prioritize their time to focus on the most important tasks and how to delegate the rest of their work to others.

Exercise: Make a to-do list every night for the following morning or every morning when you wake up. Prioritize your list in a way that outlines the most important, urgent tasks (like we discussed in Chapter 6), and put all your effort into finishing those tasks first. It sounds like common sense, but too often we ignore the most important tasks because the other less valuable things on are list are easier to complete. I often hide my phone to keep me from distracting texts, emails and Facebook messages while I'm working on my priorities. Discipline yourself to always to get your A1 task done first!

Tip: If you don't have time for your to-do list, make time. Great leaders don't watch T.V.!

3 **Great leaders cast a vision**—One of the most important jobs of a leader is to instill the team vision in everyone's minds and make everyone feel like a valuable part of the mission. When every individual is committed to the common goal and feels like they play an important role in achieving that goal, they are much more likely to work hard and enjoy the job they're doing.

Exercise: Practice saying, "I believe" when you're around your teammates—strong organizations share beliefs together. Take time to talk to your teammates about what common goals you share as a team. Is everyone on the same page and aware of what they should be working toward? Are you reaching out to each and every team member to make sure they feel welcome and comfortable within the community? Take time each week to reinforce the team vision and reach out to team members who are not as active in the community. Showing team members that you care about their success will make them feel more comfortable in the group and more motivated to continue working hard. If you have team members who come from different parts of the country or globe, it can be very useful to use social media to connect everyone. Our teams have individual Facebook groups setup so that everyone can easily connect and share with one another, no matter where they are physically.

4 *Great leaders validate their teammates and create a positive community*—Above all else, great leaders show their teammates how to be the best versions of themselves they can be. They identify their teammate's talent and validate them until their teammate has the confidence to do things they never thought were possible. My mom always says, "believe in someone before they deserve it and it will change their life."

Exercise: Make an extra effort each day to recognize a team member who might feel under appreciated or unrecognized whether it's through a phone call, email, card, or even a simple "I believe in you" text. It will take no more than a couple minutes to express this sentiment to them, but it could mean the world to the person who needs that little extra bit of support. As a matter of fact, I believe in this concept so much that I think you should make a list of everyone on your team who you directly influence. Think of your current leaders and developing leaders, and make a note of their unique talents and gifts so you can edify them regularly. Be intentional about this—once you've identified these skill sets, you can remind your leaders of them in person, via phone, via Facebook, or any other medium that can get your message across. You can never tell someone you believe in them too many times. In Shawn Achor's famous book, The Happiness Advantage, he says that committing random acts of kindness every day for 21 days can actually rewire your brain to be happier. If you can make someone else feel good, and make yourself happier in the process, what do you have to lose?

---

5 *Great leaders know the power of self-improvement and lifelong learning*—The more you know, the more you realize how much left there is to learn. As a teacher, it was always impressed upon us to be lifelong learners. I believe a true leader should be accountable for nothing less. There is always room to grow, and there is no exception to that rule.

6 **Great leaders know how to have balance**—Make sure you are scheduling time for each area of your life. Once you get into a groove with your work, it can be hard to stop and take time for yourself. Leave aside some time for just you, time for family and your kids if you have them, time with just you and your partner, time for friends and social activities, etc. What good is a leader who constantly gets burned out? You need to make time for balance. As you continue to grow as a leader and your income grows, you may also want to consider hiring help and delegating work to others so you have more time to work in the areas that require your time most.

Learning From Other Leaders

When you think about the leaders you look up to most, which qualities do you think are most important? What makes a great leader in your mind? Take a minute to create a list of characteristics that you think belong to a good leader. When you're finished, put a star next to all the qualities you believe you personally possess. Looking at the qualities that you didn't star, what is stopping you from being that kind of person? As we know from the previous chapter, anything can be achieved if you have enough discipline. If you want to become a leader, and are willing to endure all the work it will take to get there, make a commitment to yourself today that you will improve incessantly every day until you have learned to be the kind of leader that you would want to follow.

Once you've made that promise to yourself, you can start taking action toward your goal. One of the best ways you can learn to become a leader is by learning from other successful leaders in your industry. I've said it before and I'll say it again: Success leaves clues. Make sure you're shadowing and hanging out with the people who are most successful whenever you get a chance. If what they're doing is working for them, there's no reason it shouldn't work for you too! Too many people get caught up trying to reinvent the system and come up with other ways to run their business even though there has already been a successful system set-up before them—don't fall into this trap. If there is a duplicable system that has been successful for your upline, learn this system well and start putting it into action. It almost sounds too simple, but that's because all the steps have already been laid out for you. If you're still feeling unsure about how to implement your company's system for success, keep pushing yourself to work through it and learn more.

Another thing I often tell aspiring leaders is, don't wait until you have a team to start learning how to lead—start developing your skills today! One of my favorite books on leadership is The Power of Layered Leadership by Bob Goshen. If you're ever feeling unsure of your knowledge, there are two surefire ways to boost your confidence in any area: follow around the people who are good at it, and read books by experts in that subject. When you know a lot about a particular subject, you tend to feel confident talking about it. If you don't feel confident, you just need to spend more time practicing and learning. I love talking about leadership because it's a topic that I've been learning about for decades. If you're not feeling confident about your presentation or "pitch," ask someone on your team to listen and give you suggestions. When you can spit out information about the products, the system, the company, etc. without any hesitation, you're going to feel much more comfortable and you're going to enjoy it more. But, like we've said before, don't spend all your time behind a computer screen or a book if you're not spending an equal amount of time practicing that skill in action. It's better to do something and make a mistake than it is to do nothing at all.

The other great thing about leaders is that they're always willing to help those who look up to them for guidance. They know what it's like to be the underdog who is just getting started, so don't be afraid to ask for help because chances are... they asked the leaders above them for help at one time too! If you can find a leader to shadow or follow around for a couple days, that's even better. You'll be able to see how they organize their day from start to finish and get a good idea of which activities are priority tasks. Once you know what the most successful people in your industry are spending the most time on, you know that those are areas that you should be learning about and spending your time on as well.

It might be out of your comfort zone to ask someone you don't know very well for help, but if that could be the difference between your success and your failure—would you do it? It's difficult for any of us to step out of our comfort zones, but you learn the most valuable lessons in life when you're in unfamiliar territory. If you let your fears control your life and actions, you'll spend every day wondering what you could have done rather than loving what you did.

Will You Do What Others Won't?

Contrary to what many people believe, most leaders are not born leaders—leadership is a quality that tikes time to develop. The good news is you can learn it like anything else if you put in the time and effort necessary to get there. It's certainly not a job for just anyone; it requires a lot of risk, responsibility and passion, but it is a quality that can be developed if you want it badly enough. It's also a quality that can provide endless opportunities and reward—I've said it before, but I believe it bears repeating: helping other people reach their greatest potential is invaluable. If you want to feel great about yourself, you just have to make others feel great about themselves. It's an amazing feeling to know you helped someone achieve something they didn't think they were capable of. Not only that, but when you show others what's possible through leadership, they strive to become leaders themselves. And when that happens, you can build a legacy of leadership that lasts throughout your lifetime. In the next and final chapter, you're going to learn how you can raise up other leaders within your organization to create a business and income that continues growing every day, even if you're "working" at the beach.

ten.

HOW CAN I CREATE A RESIDUAL INCOME THAT LASTS A LIFETIME?

"Entrepreneurship is living a few years of your life like most people won't so you can spend the rest of your life like most people can't."

—Unknown

written by **KAMI DEMPSEY**

We know from history how important it is to have strong, ethical leaders who guide us— not only in times of abundant growth, but also in times of turmoil and uncertainty. No matter what the situation, leaders leave a positive impact on those around them. We also know how important it is to have these kinds of leaders in our businesses and organizations to ensure that each day of work runs smoothly and efficiently. We've touched on the importance of leadership in network marketing, but haven't totally explored the extraordinary impact that strong, layered leadership can have on your organization. This chapter is going to walk you through what layered leadership means and what you can do to start implementing this system of leadership throughout your teams for the kind of exponential team growth you've always dreamt of!

What is Layered Leadership?

Layered leadership is the concept of training other team members to become leaders in order to build stronger and more active teams. When you raise up leaders across your teams, they will go on to raise up leaders on their own teams— as this continues to happen, a long-lasting legacy of strong leadership throughout all of your teams will be created. This system of leadership is especially important in network marketing, because as we mentioned before, there is no one delegating work to each individual—everyone has their own business to run.

If you've ever been in this industry, you know how quickly some people can join and quit, especially when they don't feel like they're being supported by their sponsors. This can be extremely discouraging when you work hard to get people interested and excited about your business opportunity, only to have them quit a few months down the road because they didn't think they could be successful. When you train someone from each of your teams to take on a leadership role, this problem is alleviated—you retain far more team members, your teams get far more work done, and your teammates are much happier because they feel important and valuable. This sense of community makes people much more willing to go the extra mile to succeed because they know they have support behind them with each and every step they take.

Leadership is a role that came very naturally to me because of my background in teaching, coaching, and athletics, but teaching others what I knew was a whole other story—and something that excited me most. I did a great job of casting the vision and had no problem getting people excited and wanting to participate, but I did struggle to "let go" of some of my leaders because I didn't want to stop helping them before they personally felt ready to "breakaway" on their own. Denise was one of my leaders who was ready and raring to breakaway on her own soon after training—we spent a lot of time together early on, so she was able to pick up on everything very quickly. When she was ready to start leading her teams, I let her go, because I knew she was ready to take on the challenge. Other leaders, however, have wanted to hold my hand longer than they really needed to, which made it hard to turn them away when they still wanted my help. Selecting the people who would become my leaders wasn't much of a struggle for me because I've learned how to pick those people out over the years, but it may be difficult for some of you to choose the right individuals who are ready for that extra responsibility (especially early on in your business). If you find yourself having trouble deciding who you should select to start training for a leadership role, there are a couple "tests" you can do to narrow your choices down.

Who Are My Leaders?

When you instill your values and ethical actions onto those you lead every day, some people will naturally rise to the occasion and show leadership qualities when given the responsibility. The best way to know for sure whether or not certain teammates are ready for leadership is to give them a "test." Big Al Schreiter, a well-known figure in the industry, recommends that you ask your potential leaders to read a book within a few days so you can meet with them and talk about it within one week. Those who don't do it and give you excuses are likely not ready for a leadership role. Those who take on the challenge willingly and complete it, however, are probably good candidates to start giving more responsibility to. If they continue to meet or surpass your expectations as you continue giving them more responsibility, these people will be your leaders if you keep working with them. Sometimes it just comes down to a feeling too—your gut feeling won't always be right, but we all take risks every day... and some of those risks payoff big rewards.

The other cool aspect about this is that you don't always have to teach people to be leaders from scratch. Sometimes there are "leaders in disguise"—people who have all the right qualities, but haven't been in a position that allows them to use those skills effectively. I love being a talent scout and finding the people who are already leaders in their own right and then turning them onto this industry.

Remember the exercise that had you write down the characteristics of a great leader? That will come in handy again when you're trying to decide which people are best fit for the role—do they already have many of the characteristics you listed? If so, you can begin showing them how they can apply those characteristics to excel in this industry.

How Do I Start?

Once you've found the people who you want to mentor and train to become leaders, you must first let them know that you've chosen them! If your teammates look up to you and your leadership, and they feel like they've been chosen exclusively for a chance to be mentored by you, they're going to feel important and valuable. Not only that, but because they'll feel like they're the chosen few out of many other possible teammates, they will feel like you personally invested in them and their abilities, so they will be more inclined to prove their loyalty by committing to the business with everything they have. **This is important.**

When you're trying to lead an entire organization alone, it can be extremely stressful because everyone comes to think that you can just wave a magic wand and fix everything once you start solving problems for people. But once you've trained several people to lead their own teams, you can delegate some of those every day issues (product inquiries and questions, rumors about the company, etc.) to your other leaders to take care of. This will free up a lot of extra time for you to work on more important tasks, but it will also give your "leaders in training" some great experience because they'll be forced to deal with the problems that are bound to arise when they breakaway as independent leaders for their teams.

You may also want to layout a rough timeline for your leaders' "training period." Everyone will be different and learn at different paces, but you can usually expect at least a couple months of close mentoring and shadowing before your leaders will be ready to start implementing what they've learned with their own teams. When I trained leaders who wanted my help longer than they actually needed it, I figured it was fine to help them as long as they felt they needed my help. I realized later on that I was just stopping them from reaching their full potential as individual leaders when I held their hand too long. In the same vein, some of your leaders may breakaway before you personally think they're ready, but you should always let them take on more responsibility if they want to attempt. They may come back and say, "I'm not ready for that" or they might just surprise you with how much they're capable of. You should never put a lid on someone else's potential because you can't know what they will or won't do unless they have an opportunity to try.

During the "close training period," I encourage each of my leaders to travel with me to local and non-local events, listen in on my weekly calls, participate in weekly "homework," and engage in our online communities. Facebook has become an incredibly huge part of connecting our teammates from different areas together because it allows people who are thousands of miles away share life events, successes, and struggles with one another instantaneously. Weekly team calls that are separate from corporate calls are also a good idea because it allows everyone to connect and share with one another on an even more personal level. These calls also help develop the speaking skills of your leaders, which is a skill that most everyone can improve upon.

Outside of the basic engagement/participation activities, make sure you're letting your future leaders see the "behind the scenes" activities you do on a daily basis as well—for example, whenever someone on my team promotes to the next rank in our company, I make sure to recognize them in some way whether it's through a special phone call, taking them out to lunch, or sending them a card in the mail. Your leaders need to know what you're doing AND why you're doing it—all of these little tasks might not be obvious to them, so you need to make sure they're aware of them so they can practice these techniques with their own teams. A great leader needs to be aware of all of their teammates and how they're doing; is there anyone who needs a little extra help this month to hit that next promotion or someone who needs some extra support because they're having some personal problems? It might seem like a time-waster to some, but a leader who cares about each and every individual is a leader who thrives.

When you have a good grasp of who your leaders are and you've established a system of training and a timeline to do it in, you can begin training and implementing these systems. Several months of training may seem like a long time to dedicate to these people, but the work that they will take off of your hands in the long run is invaluable. You will be able to delegate to them more and more as they continue to learn, and they will begin to pick out leaders in their own teams to start the system all over again in a matter of a year or less. Once you have leaders training leaders on every level of your organization, your team will start gaining massive momentum and your paychecks (and your teammates' checks) can double, triple, and quadruple in a matter of a few months.

Because I'm a longtime athlete, I've always compared the industry of network marketing to a game of basketball. Basketball is a game of runs. The team with the most runs wins. What do I mean by runs? They go on a scoring streak. It is the same with network marketing, but we call it momentum. As your company approaches momentum or is in momentum, you are going to want systems in place specifically for creating, developing, and layering leadership. Developing leaders in the width of your business provides profitability while layering leaders in the depth of your business provides security. In a basketball game, two teams with equal levels of talent can start out even, but as soon as one team gets a few runs and picks up momentum, they can put a serious spread between them and their opponent. This is especially true if they have a few strong players who know how to work the court right off the bat. If you have strong, dedicated leaders on your team who already know how the system works and how they can recruit and train others, you will quickly outrun your competitors who have one person trying to run the whole show. This kind of organization takes more time and much more intention to build, but it will outlast and outrun any other team in the business. If your team is stacked with well-trained leaders, your team will be the champion of the league every year.

What Now?

Whether you're new to network marketing or a seasoned player in the game, I hope Denise and I have shown you how possible it is to re-dream your life when you work in this industry. Yes, it will be hard. Yes, there will be some stress. I definitely can't promise it will be easy, but I can say with certainty that it will be worth it because the rewards are endless. Instead of spending the rest of your life trading your time for money at a job you don't care about, invest in yourself and your unique, God-given talents to build a lifetime of happiness and a legacy of freedom for your family. You owe it to yourself to at least give this industry a chance—it has changed our lives forever, and we know it can change yours too if you're willing to give your full effort. It only takes a few short years of total commitment to create a passive income for generations. The only question is—are you ready to take action and start living the life of your dreams?